12-10

⊥84874

D1396705

READY
READERS

STAGE 1
PRESCHOOL-GRADE 1

Dear Parents:

Children learn to read in stages, and all children develop reading skills at different ages. **Ready Readers™** were created to promote children's interest in reading and to increase their reading skills. **Ready Readers™** stories are written on two levels to accommodate children ranging in age from three through eight. These stages are meant to be used only as a guide.

Stage 1: Preschool—Grade 1

Stage 1 stories have short, simple sentences with large type. They are perfect for children who are getting ready to read or are just becoming familiar with reading on their own.

Stage 2: Grades 1—3

Stage 2 stories have longer sentences and are a bit more complex. They are suitable for children who are able to read but still may need help.

All of the **Ready Readers™** stories are fun, easy-to-follow tales that are colorfully illustrated. Reading will become an exciting adventure. Soon your child will not only be ready, but eager to read.

Educational consultant, Wendy Gelsanliter Dore, M.A.

CONTENTS

The Rainy Day

Illustrated by J. Ellen Dolce

When it rains, Jake and his sister, Mindy, play a game. They imagine all of the things they can do when the rain stops.

"I can show you how to skate," Jake tells Mindy.

"I can show you the short cut to school," says Mindy.

"I can to dive into the sea," says Jake.

"I can ride in a balloon and look at the stars," says Mindy.

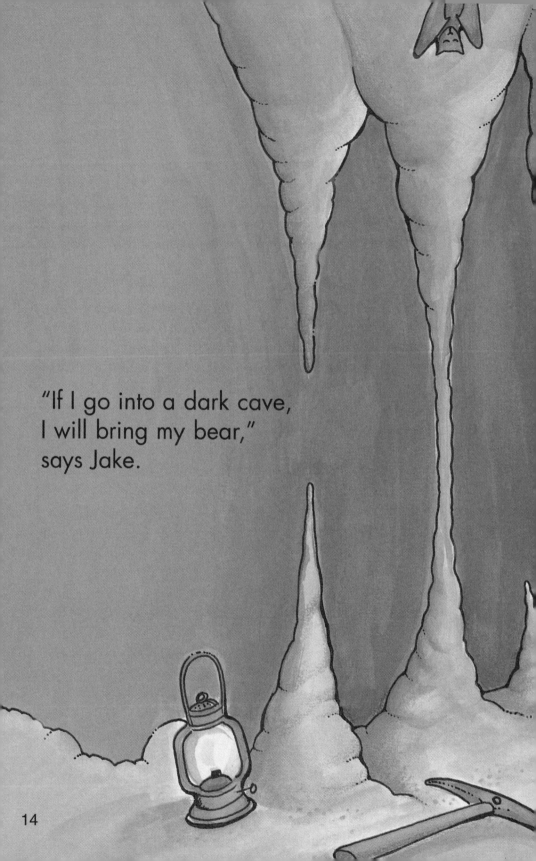

"If I go into a dark cave,
I will bring my bear,"
says Jake.

14

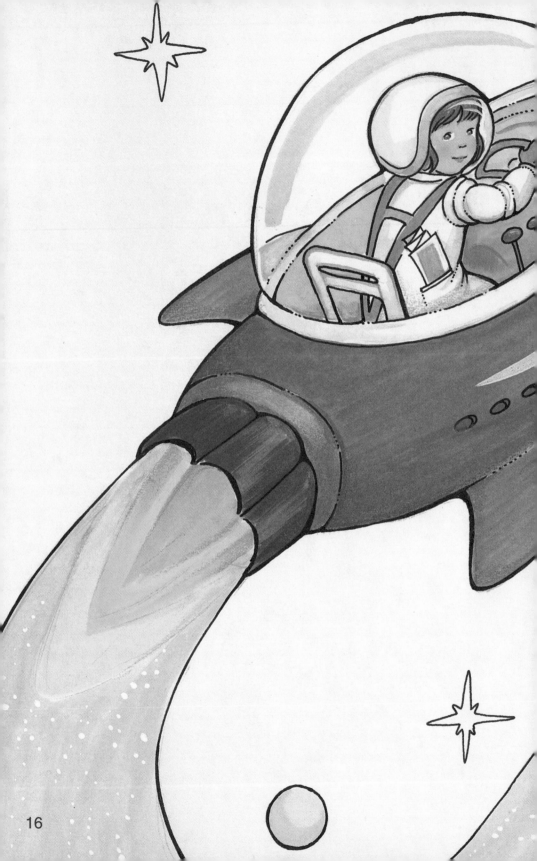

"If I go to the moon, I will ride in a rocket and go very fast," says Mindy.

"I can go ice skating with mice," says Jake.

"I can go to the park when it is dark," says Mindy.

"That will be fun," says Jake, "but bring a flashlight."

"I can dress up like a clown and walk on my hands," says Jake.

"Will you fall down?" asks Mindy.

"I can dress up like a mail carrier," says Mindy.

"I can march in my band."

"Can I be in your band?"
asks Mindy.

"I can help toads cross the road," says Mindy.

"I want to see that," says Jake.

Toad Crossing

"I think I will bake some bread, " says Jake. "Then I will put it on my head."

31

"You are funny Jake," says Mindy. "I think I will get in a train and carry animals to the circus."

Jake and Mindy imagined many fun things to do. Now it's almost time to go to bed.
"We can do some of the things we like to do tomorrow when the sun is out," says Mindy.

"Yes," says Jake. "That will be fun."

A Bunch of Balloons

Illustrated by Frank Hill

Sam and Suzy like to play together.

"What should we do today?" asks Sam.

"I want to dress up like an elephant,"
says Suzy.

"No, Suzy, we can play school.
I will be the teacher," says Sam.

"No, Sam, we can go to the circus
and see the clowns," says Suzy.

"The circus!" says Sam.
"I like the circus. Let's go."

On the way to the circus, Sam and Suzy stop at the store for some snacks. They buy cookies and candy canes.

"Look," says Sam. "There is the circus.
I will buy the tickets."

"Thank you," says Suzy.
"You are a good friend."

Sam brings Suzy a green
balloon and a hot dog.

"Watch out, Sam, there goes
the mustard," says Suzy.

Sam brings Suzy another balloon.
This one is yellow.

"Thank you, Sam," says Suzy.
"Please sit with me now."

"No, but I will be back soon," says Sam.

"I thought you would like a blue balloon
and popcorn," says Sam when he returns.

"The elephant wants popcorn, too,"
says Suzy.

When Sam brings Suzy a red balloon, she cannot hold it.

"I know where
I can put it,"
says Sam.

Sam ties the red balloon to the bow on Suzy's dress.

"Do not do that, Sam," says Suzy.

Sam does not listen to her.
He goes off to find more balloons.

Suzy floats up into the circus ring.

"I want to get down!" says Suzy.

The tightrope walker
helps Suzy down.

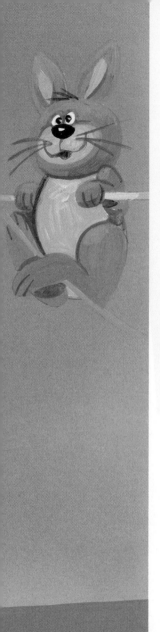

Here comes Sam.
He has more balloons.

"No more balloons, Sam.
I have enough!" says Suzy.

"But who will hold my balloons?"
asks Sam.

The hot dog vendor!

Sam and Suzy say goodbye to the tightrope
walker. What a day at the circus with
a bunch of balloons!

Best Friends

Illustrated by Valerie J. Meler

"Oh no, what a mess!
Teddy, what should we do?" asks Tommy.

"We can play as we put the toys away,"
Teddy says.

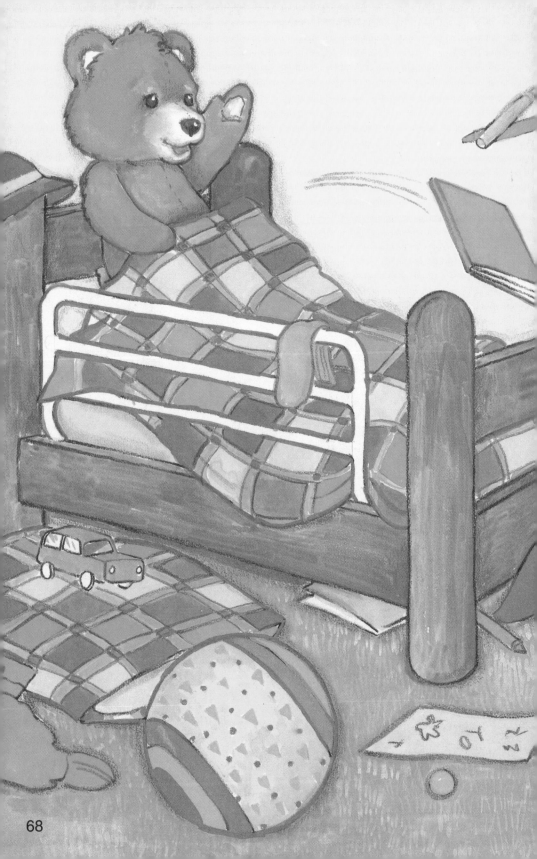

"Here is a book.
There are some blocks."

"Dust and sweep and hold your nose!"

"Let's get some toys out again!"

Tommy and Teddy like blocks.
They like planes.

"Time to eat. Wash your face, Teddy."

Tommy and Teddy set the table.

"Cake for dessert. Yummy!"

"Let's share."

Time to go to the park.
"Let's get dressed."

"Where is my shoe, Teddy?"

"I will help you turn off the light, Teddy."

"Teddy, put on your seat belt."

85

"Let's go!"

"Now it is time to read a book, Teddy."

"Good night, Teddy. You are my best friend."

"Good night, Tommy.
You are my best friend too!"

Gentle Lamb

Illustrated by Jo-Ellen Bosson

Gentle Lamb, Hungry Bear and Proud Peacock were having lunch in the forest.

"I have an idea," said Proud Peacock. "Let's have a party tonight in honor of whoever is most beautiful."

"I have a better idea," said Hungry Bear. "Let's have a party for whoever is strongest."

"Strongest? Don't be silly!" said Proud Peacock. "Who cares about being the strongest?"

Hungry Bear thought for a moment. "No, you're the silly one," he said. "Who cares about being the most beautiful?"

"Don't you make fun of me!" said Proud Peacock. "I'll come over there and peck you!"

"Peck me?" laughed Hungry Bear. "I could pick you up and throw you across the forest."

Gentle Lamb was very upset to hear her friends fighting.

"Please, please don't fight," she said. "Strong is just as good as beautiful. And beautiful is just as good as strong."

Just then, Slow Turtle walked by. Hungry Bear and Proud Peacock told him about their ideas for a party.

"But those are both silly ideas," said Slow Turtle. "We should have a party for whoever is smartest. Everyone knows that being smart, like me, is the best thing to be."

"Oh, dear," said Gentle Lamb.

"You think being smart is better than being strong?" said Hungry Bear. "Watch out, I'm going to step on you!"

Slow Turtle looked scared. Hungry Bear laughed. "See, I told you," he said.

"You think being smart is better than beautiful?" said Proud Peacock. "I am going to peck you!"

"Stop! Stop!" cried Gentle Lamb. "Beautiful and strong and smart are all good things to be. Can't we think of a party that would make everybody happy?" she asked.

Hungry Bear and Slow Turtle
went off to play ball.

Proud Peacock sat with Gentle
Lamb. "Don't be sad," he
said to her. "We'll try harder
to get along."

That night, Gentle
Lamb got a party
invitation. She put on
her best bow and
went to the forest.

On the tree was a
big sign. Gentle Lamb
read it slowly and
her eyes grew wide.

"For me?" asked
Gentle Lamb. "But
why? I am not strong
or beautiful or smart."

"Because you keep me from being a bully," said Hungry Bear.

"Because you keep me from being too vain," said Proud Peacock.

"Because you help us all to stay friends," said Slow Turtle.

"Oh, thank you," said Gentle Lamb with a happy smile. "Thank you all for being such good friends! Now we should have the party."

After the party, everyone was tired. Slow Turtle was angry. Hungry Bear had eaten the last piece of cake.

Gentle Lamb said, "Don't be angry, Slow Turtle. We can make another cake tomorrow. Let's all be friends again. It's more fun to get along than to fight."

"Yes, Gentle Lamb," everyone said. "It's much more fun to get along than to fight."

Freddie's Birthday Surprise

Illustrated by Susan Marino

Freddie is up early.
Today is a special day.
Today is Freddie's birthday.

Freddie dresses quickly.

Then he races down the stairs.

"I wonder what presents I will get for my birthday," says Freddie.

"Hi, Mom. Hi, Dad."

"Hi, Freddie."

"Where did they hide my presents?"
asks Freddie.

Freddie looks in the living room.
No presents in there.

Freddie looks in the play room.
No presents in there.

Freddie even looks behind the big clock in
the hall. No presents there, either.

No presents anywhere.

134

"There must be presents somewhere,"
says Freddie.

Freddie runs to Bobby's house.
"Bobby will have a present for me."

Bobby isn't home.

Freddie runs to Annie's house.
"Annie will have a present for me."

Annie isn't home, either.

No one is home. Freddie is sad.

"Everyone forgot my birthday," he says.

"Come home, Freddie," calls his mother.
"It's time for lunch."

Freddie walks in the door.

"Surprise! Happy Birthday, Freddie!"

There is cake. There is candy.

There are games to play.
There are presents.

All for Freddie!

One from Mom. One from Dad.

One from Bobby. One from Annie.

Freddie is happy.

What a great birthday surprise.

Happy birthday, Freddie!

Nosing For Numbers

Illustrated by Florie Freshman

We are nosing for numbers.
We are on the right track.

We will go to the toy store
and search every rack.

Nosing for numbers
can be lots of fun.
First on our list is
to find number 1.

See all the instruments.
It's time to have fun.
Look carefully now
for more number 1s.

There are dolls and a dollhouse,
all shiny and new.
If we look at them all
will we find number 2?

We will follow our noses
and hope for a clue.
You never can tell
when you will find number 2s.

Come look at the trains
and the airplanes that soar.
If we keep up our search,
we can find 3s and 4s.

Let us try over here
where they keep pogo sticks.

Keep your eyes open
to find 5 and 6.

Here are the wagons
and scooters and skates.
Do you think we will spot
any 7s and 8s?

You look on the cups,
I'll look on the plates.
That way we won't miss
any 7s and 8s.

See the toy soldiers,
all standing in line.
Maybe they know
where to find number 9.

There may be some numbers near Jack-in-the-box.
Are there any 9s near the puppets or blocks?

Let us look at the cars,
and the fire engine trucks.
We might find some 10s,
if we have any luck.

We thank you for helping us
find 1 through 10.
We hope to go nosing
for numbers again.
(Hint: look for more 10s!)

Did you find all the hidden numbers?

179

Jessie's Very Busy Week

Illustrated by Susan Mills

Jessie is always very busy. There is a lot to do every day of the week!

Monday morning, Jessie and Mom go shopping together. What kind of store do they go to?

After shopping with Mom, Jessie and his friend Sam play with cars.

Tuesday is a very special day. Jessie gets to buy a puppy!

Which one would you buy?

Can you see the new puppy? The new puppy paints! Jessie paints too.

Jessie and the puppy play with a fire truck. What a fun Tuesday!

Wednesday, Jessie makes cookies.
What do you like to make?

Thursday morning, Jessie plays outside in the garden. He likes to smell the flowers.

Thursday night, Jessie plays inside. What toy should he play with?

Friday is the day Mom buys fruit. Jessie likes bananas. What fruit do you like?

Saturday, Jessie goes to Grandpa's farm! He sees pigs and chickens. What do you see?

Later, when it gets hot, Jessie puts on shorts and goes down to the pond. How many fish does Jessie see?

Sunday, Jessie and his Mom and Dad have a party. It's Mom's birthday.

At night, Jessie has a bubble bath with his
duck and his boat.

It is Monday morning again.
Look at Jessie! What will he do
today? What will you do?

What Friends Do

Illustrated by Valerie J. Meler

There are many things that friends
can do each day.

It is fun to camp out in a tent.

It is fun to sail boats.

It is fun to play with a ball at the beach.

Friends like to build with blocks.

Friends like to fly kites.

Friends can look at fish.

Friends can have a picnic in the grass.

Friends can pick flowers.

Friends like to draw letters.

It is always fun when friends ride bikes.

It is fun to roller-skate.

Friends like to catch butterflies.

Friends like to jump rope.

At night, friends like to catch fireflies.

And before bedtime,
friends can look at the stars.

Winston Finds a Treasure

Illustrated by Frank and Carol Hill

Winston Walrus lives in a funny old house
by the sea.

One day, in the attic, he found his Uncle Bluewhiskers' old red pirate boots.

"These are great!"
Winston thought as
he put them on. "I bet
Uncle Bluewhiskers
misses his old red
pirate boots."

Then, one
of the toes
popped open
and out fell a
treasure map!

Winston called his friend Saul.

"We are going on a treasure hunt," he said.
"Meet me at the wharf right away."

On the way to the wharf, Saul saw his friends Wilma Whale and her daughter, Paul Pelican, Sally Seagull and Sid Starfish.

At the wharf, Winston showed Saul the map. "This must be the lost treasure that Uncle Bluewhiskers always talks about," Winston said.

257

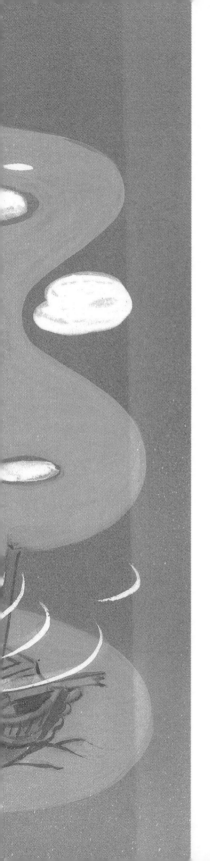

When they reached the place where X marked the spot on the map, the friends could see an old ship under the water.

Winston and Saul jumped into the water and swam down to the ship.

There, in the middle of the ship, was a pirate chest. They opened it right away...

...and found Uncle Bluewhiskers' pet goldfish, Treasure!

"So that is what
Uncle Bluewhiskers
meant when he
said he had lost
his treasure,"
yelled Winston.

All of the sea creatures swam over
when they heard the noise.

"This is a lucky day, Winston. Uncle
Bluewhiskers will be so happy," Saul said.

Saul and Winston got into the boat and rowed back to the wharf.

As they walked home, they heard Uncle
Bluewhiskers call to them.

"Where did you find my goldfish? I thought I would never see him again!" he said.

Then Uncle Bluewhiskers gave Winston and Saul some gold. "Thank you," they said.

"Wow! Treasure after all!" said Winston as he and Saul ran off to buy some ice cream.

Later, Winston and Saul went to see Uncle Bluewhiskers and his Treasure. What a lucky day for all!

Animal Antics

Illustrated by Kathleen Smith-Fitzpatrick

Look at the animal babies.
They like to have fun.

The kittens play games all day in
the bright sun.

The lambs run and kick the can, a game they often play.

The puppies tell funny jokes every
night and day.

The chicks run to look at Mama Bear
and her pie.

The kittens try to climb a tree and one climbs up too high.

Mama Bear sees the chicks and says,
"Go away from here."

The kitten runs to Mama Cat, glad
that she is near.

While puppies roll on the floor and sing a little song.

The chicks run off with the pie and it's gone before too long.

Mama Bear will know that the chicks
ate the pie.

Tiny footprints are all over, and chicks are running by!

Now all the animal babies have a
story to tell.

About the day the chicks ate too much pie. . .

. . . they didn't feel so well!

Bye-bye for now, the animal babies say.
Tomorrow we'll have more games to play.